The Amazing World of Underwater Photography

by
Beverly Rosenthal
and
Jeffrey S. McDonald

Contemporary **cpi** Perspectives, Inc.

This book is distributed by Silver Burdett Company, Morristown, New Jersey 07960

Library of Congress Number: 83-60110

Photo Credits

Photos courtesy of Beverly Rosenthal
Every effort has been made to trace the ownership of all copyrighted material in this book and to obtain permission for its use.

Manufactured in the United States of America
ISBN 0-89547-092-6

Contents

Chapter 1

Snorkeling— A Visit to Another World

The red sun seems to rise out of the ocean. Its rays brighten the sandy beach of a tropical island. Beads of light skip across a blue-green ocean so clear you can see to its bottom. And there, a completely different world awaits those who are lucky enough to visit.

A small group of people makes its way to the water's edge. They look to the rising sun, and then out across the water. Filled with excitement, each seems to sense the beauty and splendor that lies below the water's surface.

In a matter of minutes, these men, women, and children will become strange-looking creatures, no longer able to walk easily on land. They push their feet into black flippers. They pull masks over their heads. They buckle white life belts around their waists. These people are getting ready for the thrill of a lifetime—a

4   A world of incredible beauty awaits the snorkeler.

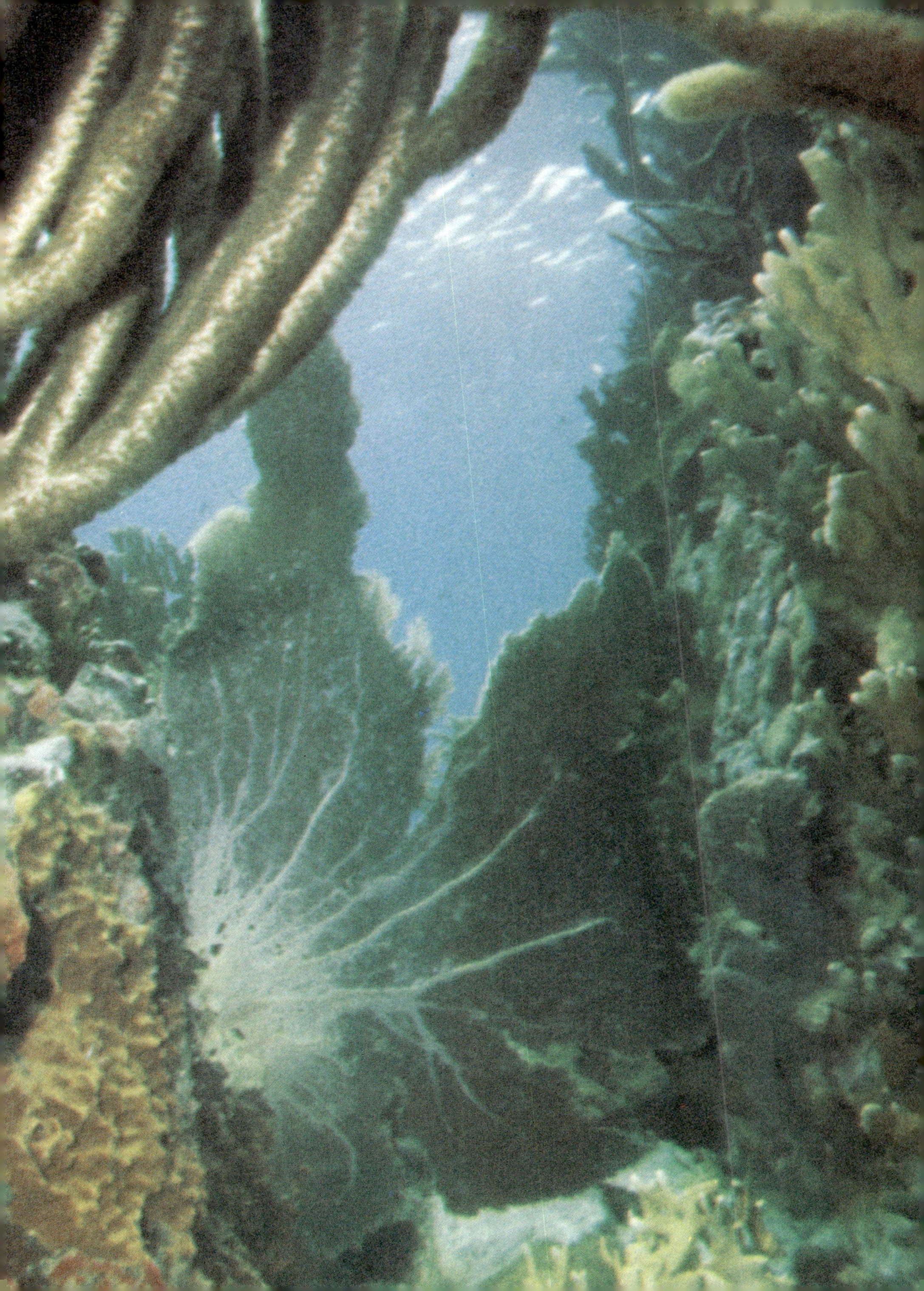

simple sport called *snorkeling*. Although they can no longer walk well on land, they will soon glide with ease through the ocean. And there they will enter a world that is home to an unbelievable array of strange creatures—creatures that most of these people have never seen before.

Before the snorkelers leave land, each slings a small black camera case around his or her neck. The camera can be the snorkeler's most precious piece of equipment. The snorkeler's camera is designed to take pictures of the living world underwater. Standing in the water, the swimmers pull at the black snorkeling tube attached to the side of their masks. They insert the flattened, oval end of the tube into their mouths. Then, in teams of two, they begin to float, face down, in the clear sea.

The sport of snorkeling would seem strange to people in some parts of the world. But on this tropical island, no one is surprised to see this group swimming and flipping its way toward an underwater reef. Moving smoothly, just under the surface of the water, the snorkelers' clear face masks help them view the scene below. Through their black snorkeling tubes, they can breathe underwater. The curved tubes run from their mouths to the air above the surface.

One of the great things about snorkeling is that anyone can do it well—people old and young, small and large, male and female. And once they get a taste

Snorkeling gear helps the swimmer to move smoothly through the water.

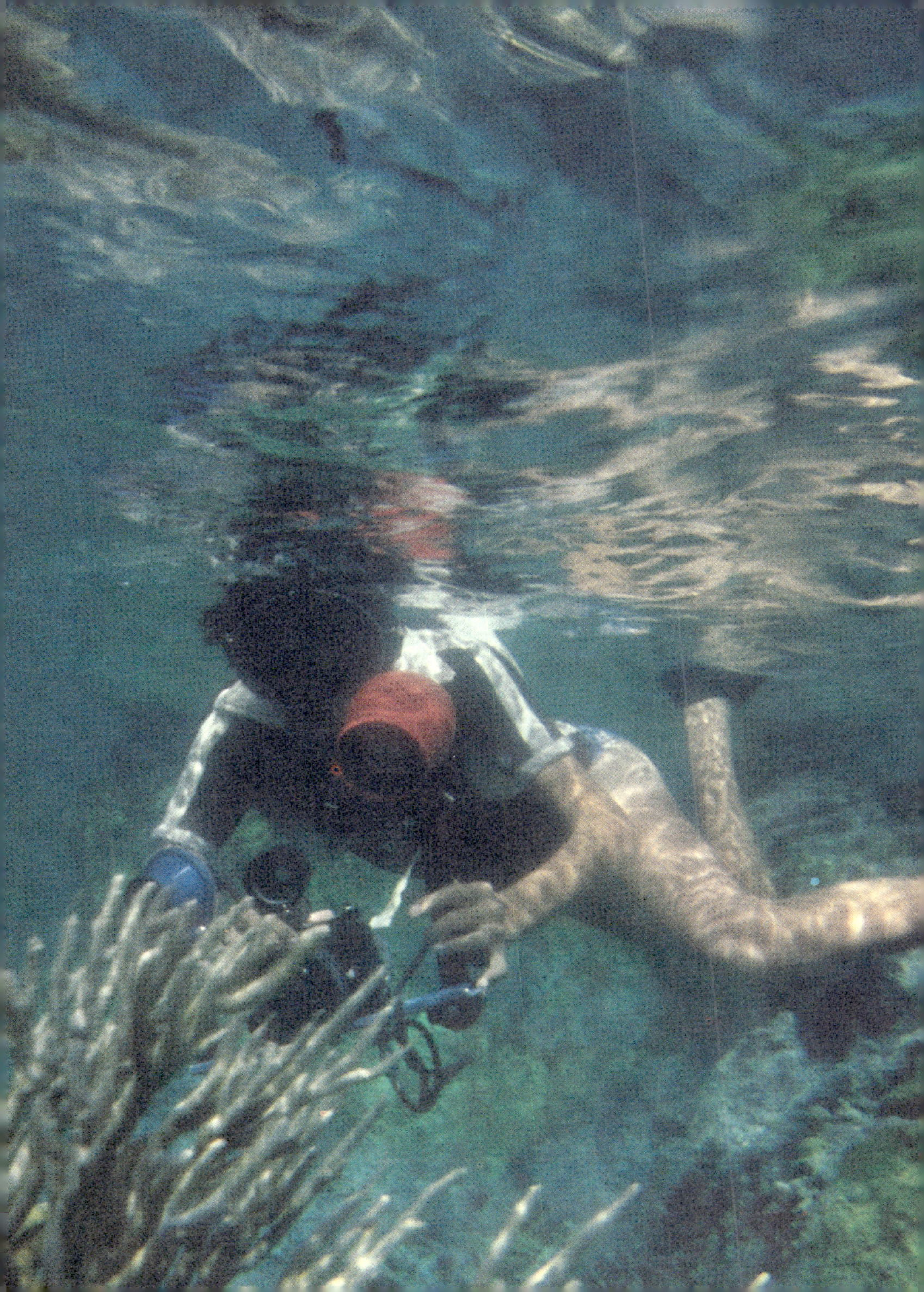

of the sport, people usually become avid snorkeling fans. This is no wonder, for snorkeling is fun almost anywhere—in a lake, in a river, even in a swimming pool. Of course, any ocean snorkeler who glimpses the fantasyland beneath the waves immediately understands why people like to record the experience with their special cameras.

If you have never tried the sport yourself, you might like to learn to snorkel. And once you have learned to snorkel well, you too can become an underwater photographer. This book can help you to begin enjoying one of the world's most thrilling sports. It will describe the simple equipment you will need, and the techniques you should use. It will also let you peek at just a few of the sights in the amazing world that awaits you and your camera under the water.

If you are seriously thinking about taking pictures underwater, here are a few facts you may want to think about. Talented underwater photographers are among the highest paid "shutterbugs" in the world. These men and women work mostly on their own, or for magazines and photo services. A sharp, clear, and truly unusual undersea shot may sell for thousands of dollars.

Of course, becoming a professional underwater photographer takes great skill and courage, plus years and years of hard work. It is not for everyone.

There are, however, many amateur underwater

photographers. They pursue the hobby just for its thrill and fascination. They have become "hooked" on the rhythms of the sea, and on the many beautiful and mysterious living secrets it holds. To the amateur, snorkeling and underwater photography are simple and inexpensive hobbies that can be inspiring, educational, and relaxing.

Some pictures in this book were taken by young people, often not yet in their teens, using inexpensive, watertight cameras. They began taking pictures just the way you would. And, just as you can become a skilled underwater photographer, you will see that these young people were able to get great results in recording some of the colorful forms of underwater life they discovered. These young people did not have to travel in space to visit another world. They found one right beyond the water's edge.

One of the most popular targets for underwater photographers is the coral reef. Coral is an organism that attaches itself to the ocean floor. It also attaches itself to submerged trees, rocks, and even sunken ships. It then multiplies and very rapidly covers a large area. The barrier reef off Australia, for example, covers 1,250 miles along that country's coast. There are many types of coral, each with its own color and pattern. The photographs in this book were all taken around just one such coral reef.

Snorkelers also find many other exciting underwater

areas to visit. These include rocky ledges, seaweed beds, riverbanks, and sunken lake logs in which different fish have made their homes. Coral reefs are dream worlds for most snorkelers because coral itself can be so colorful. Also, a coral community attracts some of the world's strangest and most interesting creatures.

Fish and other sea creatures are attracted to coral because food and shelter on the reef are usually abundant. So many creatures living together, however, must become quite competitive. They compete with one another for available food. Some of the competitors are parasites. A parasite lives on other living creatures without giving anything in return. Some parasites, for example, live in the bodies of animals feeding on the food its host eats. Sea parasites attach themselves to fish, but usually do not cause their hosts any harm. When the host fish is harmed, the parasite may lose its free meals. There are other organisms that indirectly help each other meet their needs. Neither organism could live as well without the other. There are so many different living arrangements in the world of coral that the reef provides a constant source of surprise and wonder for snorkelers and underwater photographers. There is always something new to see and photograph.

Chapter 2
Selecting Your Equipment

The beginning underwater photographer needs only a few pieces of equipment. Unlike scuba equipment, snorkeling equipment can be bought fairly inexpensively. All of it is easy to use. Gear for snorkeling is lightweight. This helps make moving from place to place and taking pictures underwater safe and enjoyable.

Here are six basic pieces of equipment needed for snorkeling and taking underwater pictures.

1. *The Mask.* The mask has a clear plastic window that covers your eyes and nose. It is fitted to your head by an adjustable elastic headband. A rubber seal around the window presses against your face to keep water away from your eyes and nose. A mask with a smaller window will probably fit best. Be sure it will give you a watertight seal. You can make certain the mask fits your face by following these simple steps:

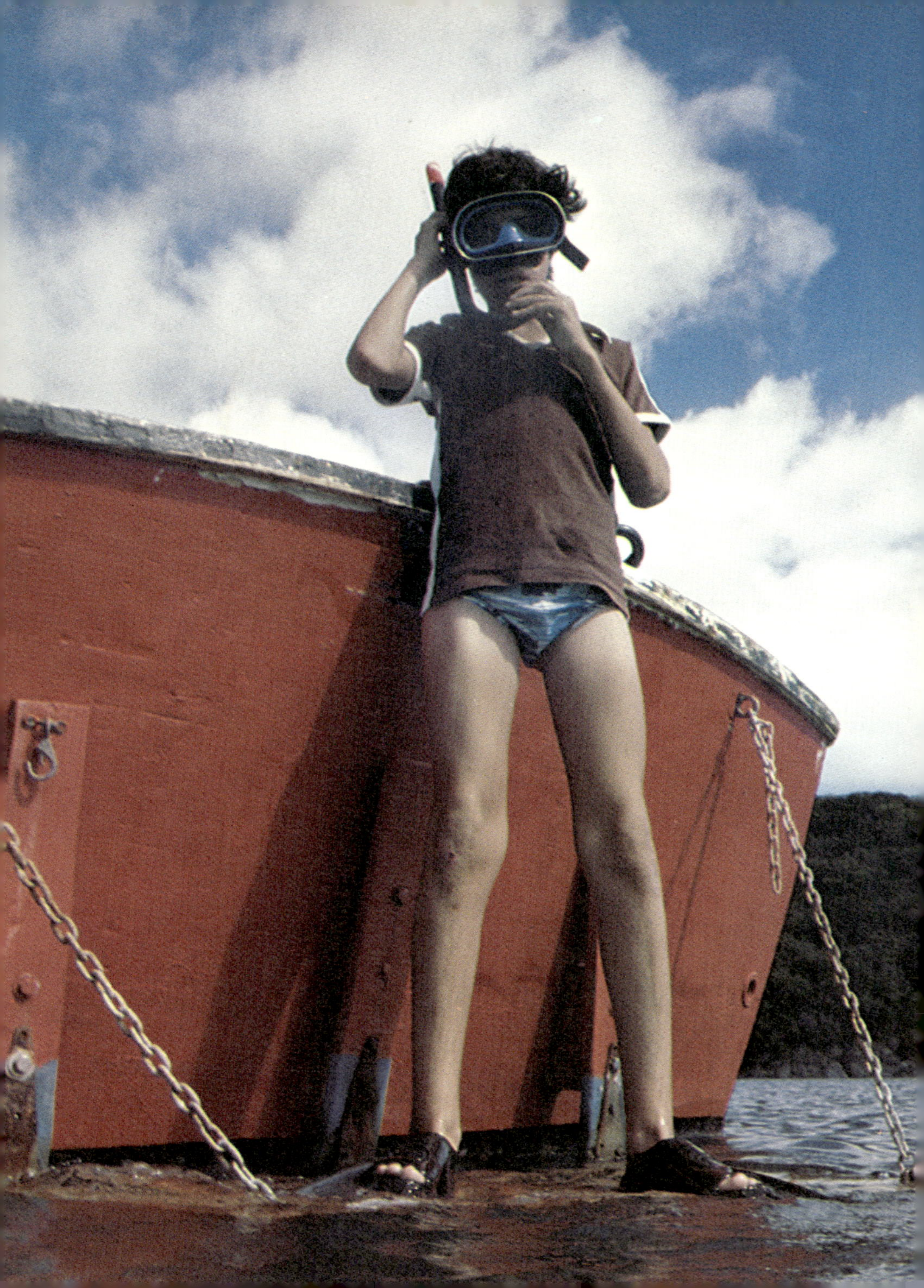

Step 1—Rest the mask, window down, on the flat
       palm of your hand.
Step 2—Lower your face against the mask until
       your face presses tightly against the rubber
       seal all around the mask. Still holding the
       mask tightly against your face, raise your
       head.
Step 3—Keep your mouth closed and breathe in
       hard, through your nose only. While you
       are breathing in, take your hand from the
       mask. If the mask stays against your face
       while you are breathing in through your
       nose, the mask will give you a good seal in
       the water.

A double-sealed mask is best, but a simple one is
fine and should cost as little as $12.00.

2. *The Snorkel.* A snorkel is a curved plastic breathing
   tube. It has a rubber flap that fits inside your
   mouth. By keeping your lips closed around this
   rubber end, you can keep water out and breathe
   easily through your mouth. Of course, the open
   end of the curved tube must always remain above
   water. When you want to dive, all you need to do is
   hold your breath. Once you resurface, you can clear
   the snorkel of water simply by blowing out through
   your mouth. The snorkel is kept in place by an
   adjustable strap attached to your mask.

The proper equipment is a must.

3. *The Fins* (Flippers). Fins are made of rubber, and should fit snugly on your feet. Their width and length give you added moving power in the water. Fins resemble the feet of a duck. They are solid and webbed. You can swim much faster and farther with flippers than you can simply by kicking your feet. Choose fins that are light in weight. For example, do not use scuba fins. They are too heavy and awkward for snorkeling. You should be able to buy a good pair of fins for under $20.00.

4. *The Camera.* Depending upon how much money you have to spend, you can waterproof a regular camera with a special plastic bag, or you can buy a special underwater camera. The special plastic bag for an ordinary camera is called a Marine Bag. It costs about $25.00 and fits just about any camera. Professional photographers use very expensive, carefully designed camera equipment. But for under $100.00, a beginner can choose from many waterproof cameras now on the market.

5. *The Flotation Belt.* Even snorkelers who swim well will benefit by wearing a life belt or jacket when snorkeling. Such a personal flotation device provides more than safety in snorkeling. It is also important to be relaxed and comfortable underwater. The personal flotation device will help you save energy and concentrate on the strange world around you.

6. *The Strobe.* Sometimes the underwater photographer wants to shoot a subject in an area where there is little light available. This calls for a watertight strobe light. Many strobes are lightweight and easy to handle. They give off a powerful beam of light that can often make the difference between dull, muddy pictures and bright, sharp ones. Beginners need not start out with a strobe. This piece of equipment should be added after you become skilled at taking pictures under normal lighting conditions.

These six pieces of equipment are all you need to begin snorkeling and taking pictures underwater. The easy-to-use equipment enables you to enter a world that is normally unreachable. When you have learned the few techniques described in the next chapter, you will have no trouble entering this fascinating world.

Chapter 3
Getting Ready To Explore

Of course, learning to snorkel will be most fun if you live in a tropical region where coral reefs abound. Picture taking, too, will be more fun, right from the beginning. Many people, however, do not live near tropical beaches and coral reefs. They find other ways to get the most from underwater photography. Lakes, rivers, and deep streams all have strange secrets you can uncover. Large tidal pools left by the changing ocean tides often offer a safe area in which to snorkel. Tidal pools are usually a haven for a number of plants and animals.

A swimming pool can be a good place to learn how to take underwater pictures. Your pictures may not be very interesting, but you can certainly learn to snorkel and handle a camera in a pool. You can also learn how to make the best use of available light by snapping underwater pictures in a swimming pool.

Keeping Your Mask Clear

In the last chapter you learned to select a face mask that will fit comfortably and provide a watertight seal. Selecting the best fitting mask may be your most important step in learning to snorkel. A mask that lets water in can ruin the fun of snorkeling.

Keeping the plastic window of the mask clear is also important. The window may cloud over while you are in the water. This annoying fog is caused by your warm breath condensing on the inside of the cooler window. You can prevent much of this condensation by spitting on the inside of the window before putting on your mask. Rub the saliva all over the window. Then adjust the headstrap to keep the rubber mask seal tight around your face.

Breathing Through the Snorkel

The snorkel is quite easy to use. Place the rubber flap in your mouth, and hold it in place with your teeth. Make sure to keep your lips tight around the mouthpiece. This gives you a clear passage to the air above the water. Be sure to keep your lips closed and breathe only through your mouth.

The snorkel will reach the air above the water as you swim just under the surface. You will have to get used to swimming along at just the right height so that the snorkel remains safely above the water.

Using Your Fins

Before putting your fins on, submerge them under the water. This will help you slide them on and keep them tight on your feet. It is difficult to walk normally with fins. The easiest way to cope with this problem is to walk backwards into the water.

When swimming with fins, keep your legs straight, and move them from the hips. Point your toes as straight as you can, and move the fins up and down so they push you along in the water. Use a *gentle* kicking action. Remember that your fins are meant to help you save your strength, not use it up.

Your flotation belt or life jacket should be snug enough to stay on in the water, but not so tight as to make breathing difficult.

You should have all your equipment in place before you enter the water. It is difficult to put on your mask and fins while trying to stay afloat.

Making Snorkeling Safe Fun

Before learning to snorkel, learn to swim. Your local "Y" or a high school may offer Red Cross swimming instruction. Even good swimmers should study their swimming areas. Find out about underwater rocks and currents in the water you choose for swimming. Always have an adult watch you, and go snorkeling with someone else who can swim.

18

Snorkeling

Start snorkeling in shallow water, until you feel comfortable with your equipment and know how it should be used. You should also start snorkeling without your camera in hand. Once you are familiar with the rhythm and feel of snorkeling, you will be able to give your full attention to taking pictures.

Float face down in the water, breathing air into and out of your mouth through the snorkel tube. Do not breathe through your nose at all. Let your arms float on the surface, and keep your head down so you can look around at the world beneath you. Above all, *relax*!

The best snorkelers are completely relaxed in the water. They do not move their arms as they would when swimming regularly. They gently kick their fins to push themselves through the water. You know you are relaxed in the water when your breathing is regular, when you do not feel tired from trying to stay afloat, and your legs do not cramp from kicking too hard.

You will find that snorkeling is easy to master. Once you reach the motion you want, you are ready to capture some of the sights below with your waterproof camera.

Whether you would like to take underwater pictures of your friends in a pool, or focus in on a colorful fish, the following points will help you get good results.

You should use fast film in your camera, either *ASA 200* or *400*. If you are not familiar with cameras, do not let labels or terms scare you. Fast film is simply film that is very sensitive to light. It lets you take pictures in dark or shadowy areas. This film is useful because sunlight is filtered as it goes through water. But some sunlight does reach the ocean bottom. Fast film will help you use the sunlight that is available.

You should keep the lens opening of your camera small. Set a slow shutter speed—about 1/60 of a second. These camera controls—*lens opening* and *shutter speed*—regulate the camera's intake of light. They determine which objects will be in focus in your picture. These techniques are best learned by actually handling the camera. Don't be afraid to experiment— this is the best way to learn.

When photographing underwater, it is important to be patient and look for details. Many forms of life use *camouflage* to hide themselves from their enemies. This means they blend in with their surroundings so they can not easily be seen. The more you examine an area, the more details you will see. Before long, you may pick up some interesting movements that you would not normally notice.

As with all photography, it is important to keep your camera steady. Even a slight movement can cause a picture to blur. The water will give you added support for aiming your camera at a subject. It is also a good

     Many kinds of cameras can be used underwater.

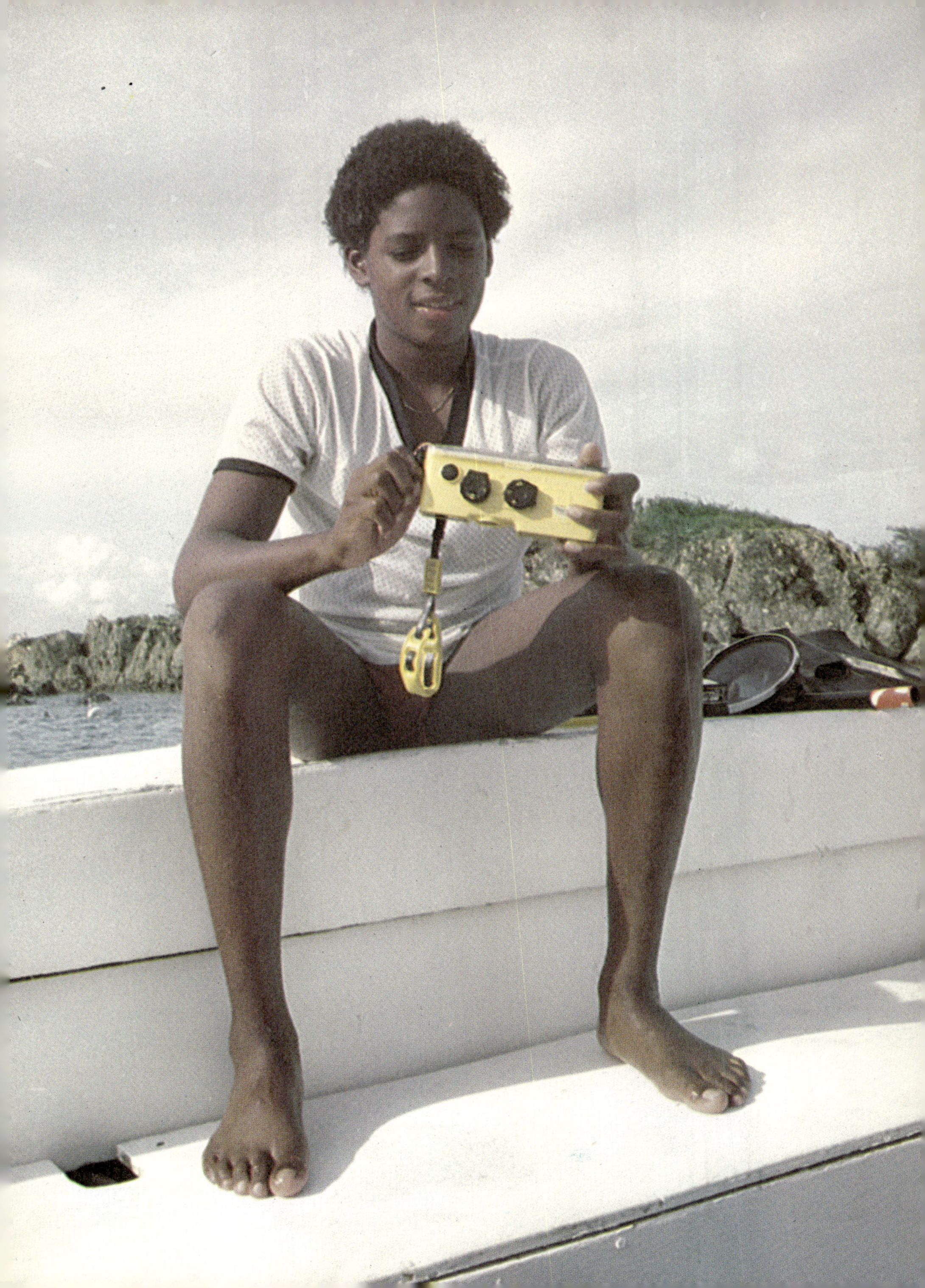

idea to avoid very fast-moving subjects, since these will often appear as a blur in your picture.

By extending your arms and body, you can angle your camera to photograph an interesting plant or fish. This is what the girl on page 23 is doing. You should also remember to frame your shots. If an object is wide or is swimming horizontally, you can photograph it by keeping the camera in its normal position. If you photograph a tall object, hold your camera so that your subject will be framed vertically.

If you are not sure you have enough light for a picture, or if you have too much light, then photograph the same subject several times using different light exposures. This will ensure that you will have just the right amount of light to get a clear picture. When using a strobe, set it before you get close to your subject. Then you will not have to make unnecessary moves that could scare your subject away.

Concentrate on getting within three or four feet of the subject you are photographing. This will bring out details and colors in your pictures. Many creatures in the sea are timid and small, so you will have to move slowly in order to see them and not scare them off.

It is usually best to shoot your pictures so that the camera lens is pointed straight at your subject, rather than down toward the bottom. This will give your pictures a better lighted, more interesting background. The picture on page 25 is of a type of coral. The

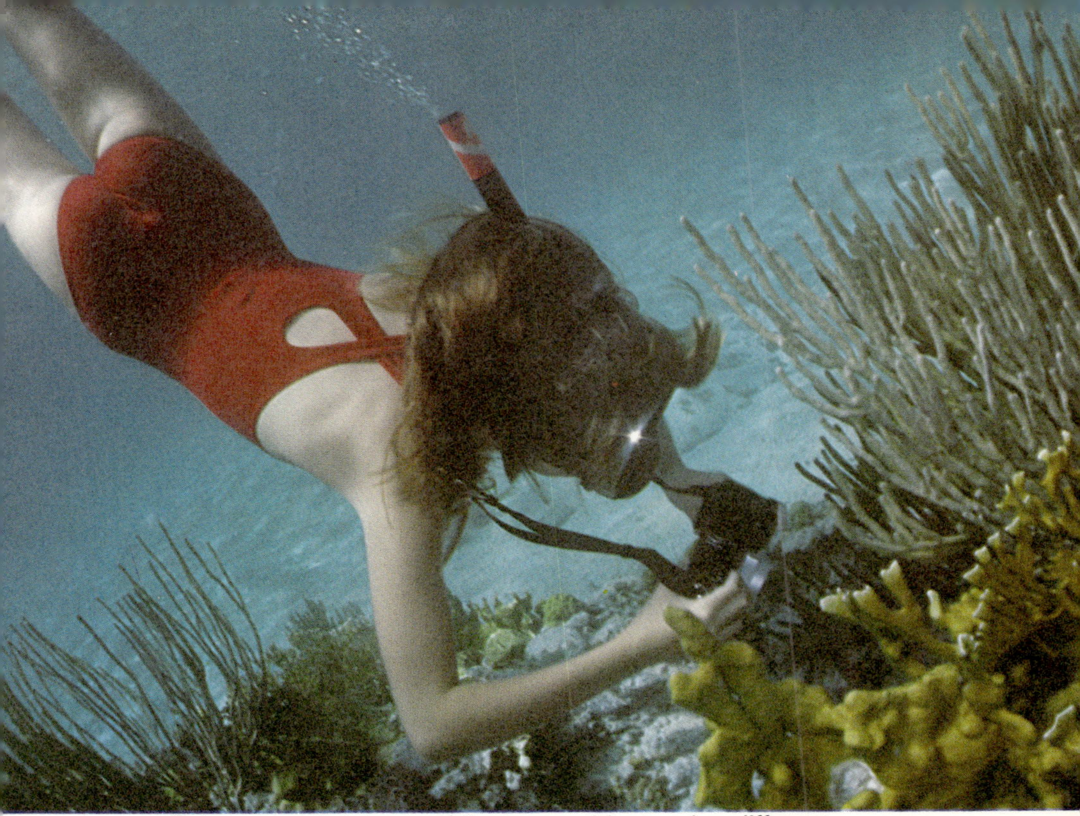

Take several pictures of the same object, using different camera settings.

photographer was able to create the interesting silhouette effect by shooting into the sunlight above the water's surface.

Once you become familiar with an underwater camera, you can add special lenses for added effects. These lenses range from wide angle lenses to telephoto lenses. The wide angle lens gives you a broader view of the sea. The telephoto lens brings your subjects closer by magnifying them. The lens you choose will depend on the kinds of pictures you like to take. While you are

23

learning, using the regular lens already on your
camera will produce satisfactory results. Most of the
pictures in this book were taken with such basic lenses.

Snorkeling is a safe sport when people are careful.
However, there are sometimes creatures in the water
that make the sport *seem* frightening. Most of these
creatures are not harmful if people respect rather than
provoke or threaten them.

One fearsome creature of the sea is the legendary
shark. But sharks are rarely seen in shallow waters or
around reefs. Also, most sharks avoid human
swimmers. The snorkeler who respects the shark is
careful not to swim where anyone is spearfishing, and
avoids garbage-polluted waters. The wise snorkeler
also avoids snorkeling at night.

Barracudas are ferocious-looking fish, mainly
because of their razor-sharp teeth. They grow to be
about three or four feet long, but they are timid.
Barracudas prey on small, shiny fish. Snorkelers who
respect barracudas remember not to wear anything
flashy, such as jewelry, in the water. A barracuda might
be attracted to the reflection.

Rays are shy, gentle creatures. One of the many
rewards of snorkeling is to see them gliding gracefully
near the floor of the ocean. Some rays have barbed
tails. Since they often burrow in the sand, make sure
you are careful where you step.

Eels usually come out at night. They live in holes in

          Shooting into the light can create interesting effects.

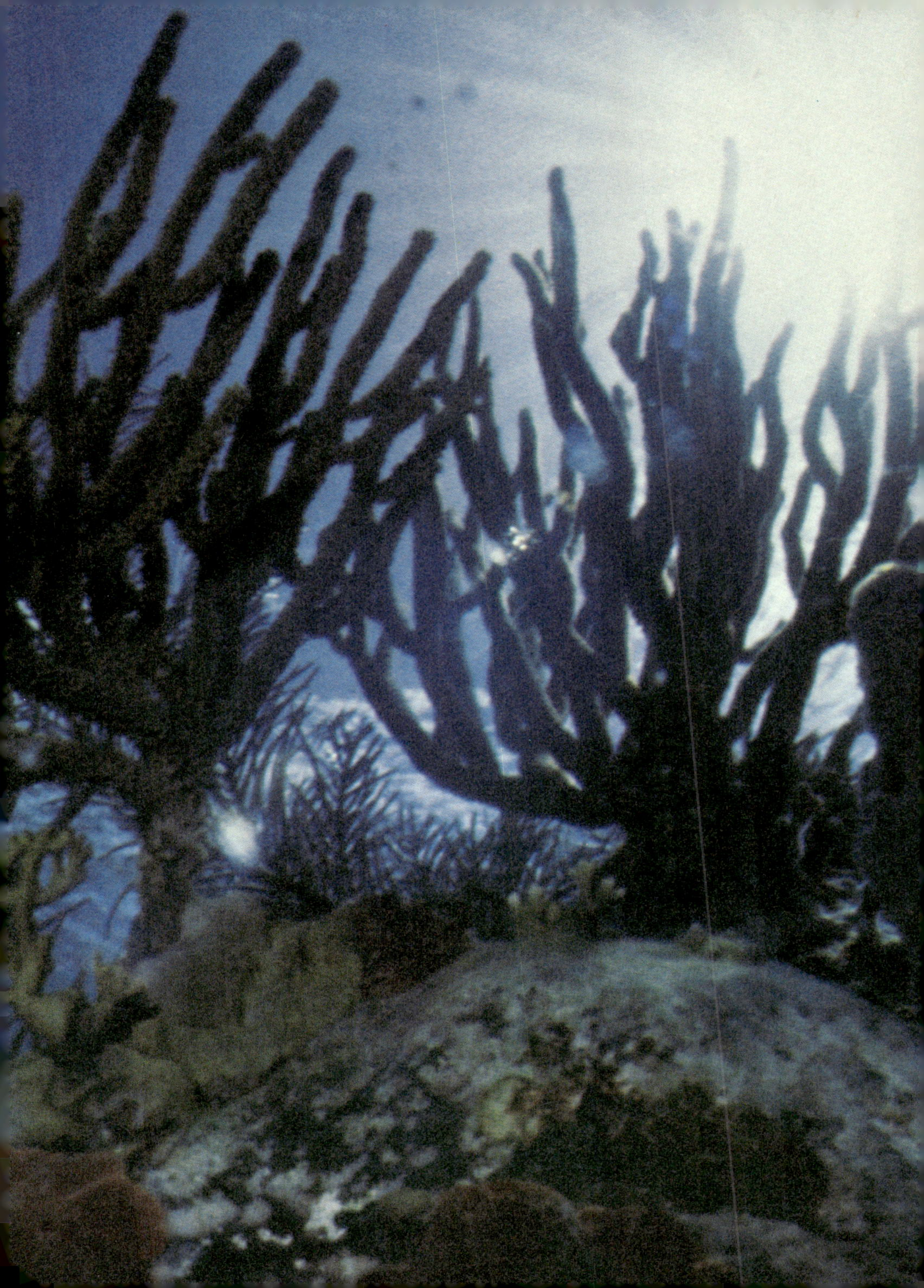

coral and rocks during the day. They will not attack or bite unless threatened. When snorkeling around coral reefs, do not stick your hands inside any openings or probe into hidden areas.

The strange-looking *octopus* is also a very timid creature. It will flee when approached, and does not present any real danger to a snorkeler.

Some small sea creatures can inflict painful wounds on the snorkeler who shows them too little respect. *Sea urchins,* for example, such as the one shown on page 27, can be picked up very gently. But do not handle a sea urchin roughly. Its spines are sharp, to ward off a sea enemy's attack. If you do get pricked by a sea urchin's spine, the pain will be mild and will not last long.

Fire coral has stinging cells that burn your skin if you brush against it. This pain is also mild and short-lived. Bristle worms are small worms that crawl over rocks and coral. If you touch one, its bristles might stick, producing a slight sting.

Snorkelers are safe as long as they do not take unnecessary chances by trying to reach into holes and hidden areas, or touch unknown plants or animals.

By following a few rules and techniques, anyone can learn how to snorkel in just a few outings. There is very little preparation needed for this exciting exploration of a world teeming with unusual and beautiful forms of life.

The spines of the sea urchin are very sharp and must be handled carefully.

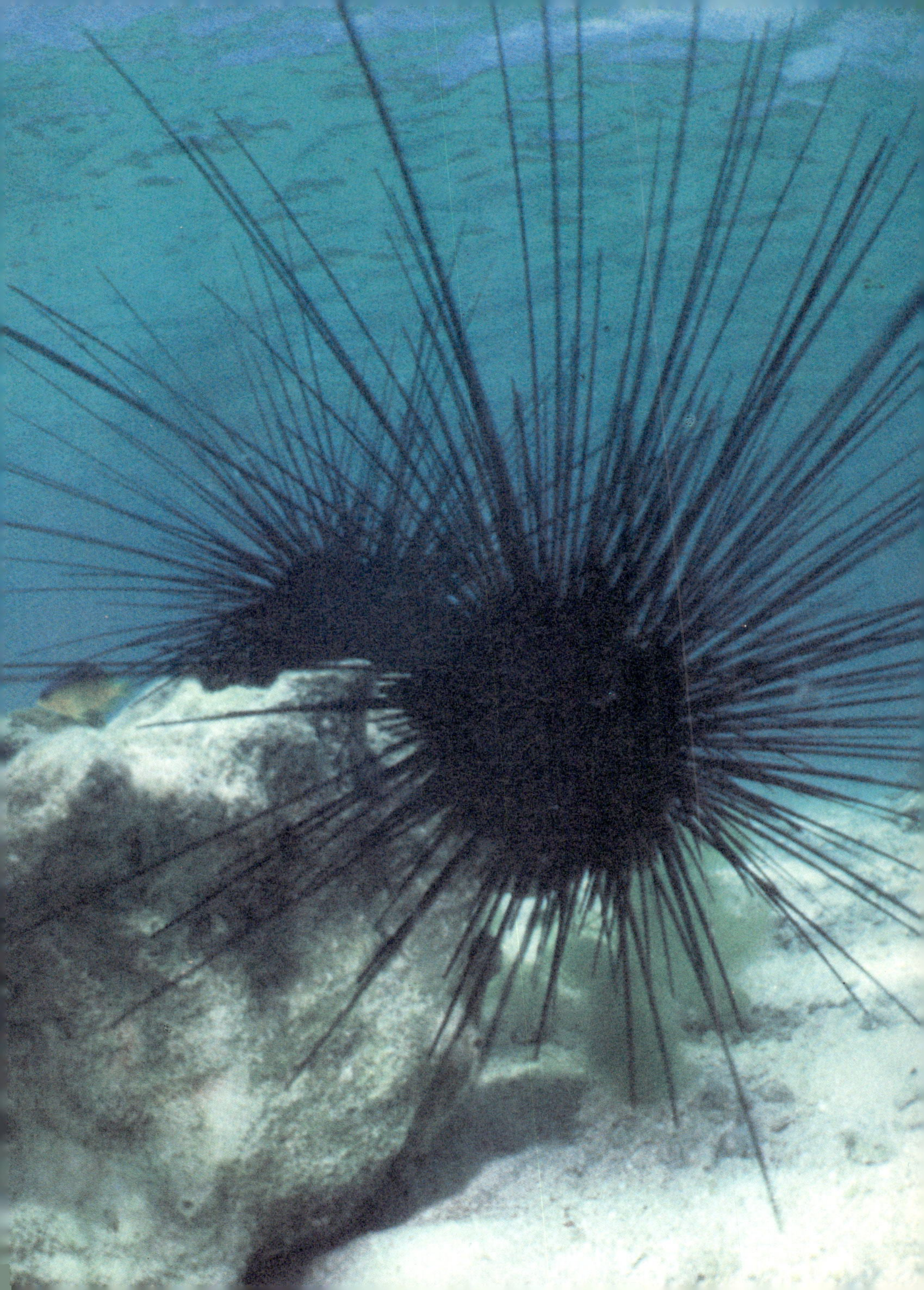

Chapter 4

Exploring a Strange New World

Coral is found in warm, shallow waters where sunlight and oxygen are available. It is one of the most spectacular forms of life in the ocean. There are a great many varieties of coral. Some coral is brightly colored, and grows into unusual and beautiful shapes. Coral beds can stretch from a few feet to many miles.

Coral is actually a type of animal. However, it provides such an attractive home for plants that it is considered an important part of the garden of the sea. Coral even spreads by producing buds. The *elkhorn coral* shown on page 29 is in the process of budding. These stalks of coral will quickly grow to over five feet in length. It will take on shapes that actually resemble the horns of an elk.

The shapes of corals are more than strikingly beautiful. They are also necessary to the survival of many sea creatures. They provide protection, food,

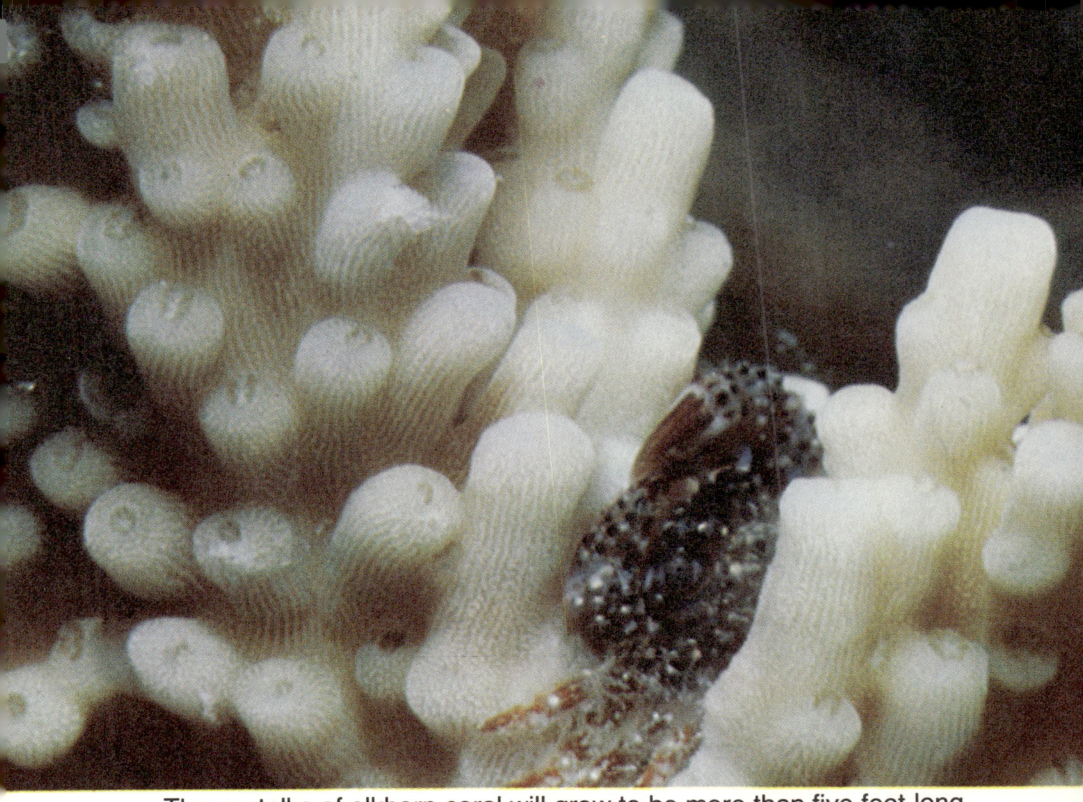

These stalks of elkhorn coral will grow to be more than five feet long.

and living space for a great many fish and plants. The law of life for sea creatures is much the same as it is on land. Creatures survive by finding enough to eat and by avoiding being eaten themselves. The holes and caverns formed by coral serve as safe hiding places for many species of sea life. Look again closely at the picture on this page. Do you see a small crab hidden in the tentacles of the coral? This is a good place for a crab to hide from its enemies. While the crab is protected and difficult to see, it can grab food particles called plankton from the water.

The buds grown by coral are called *polyps.* Plankton
enters coral through the polyps, where it is processed
as food. The picture on page 31 shows the polyps of
a blue coral. Inside these polyps reside many forms
of plant life. Small plants thrive on coral because coral
grows best where there is enough sunlight for plankton
to live. Also, coral produces carbon dioxide as a by-
product of its use of plankton. The plants give off
oxygen, which the coral needs to survive. It seems that
plants and coral have adapted to one another, creating
conditions needed for both to go on living.

As a bed of coral continues to grow, the coral at the
center of the bed begins to die. This happens because
the coral center receives less sunlight and oxygen. The
dead coral forms the solid base on which new coral and
other forms of life can flourish.

The coral reef is one of nature's most colorful
displays. It is also an important part of the balance
struck between creatures of the sea.

One of the fish often found around a coral reef is
the *trunkfish.* As you can see from the picture on page
32, the trunkfish is a very unusual-looking creature. It
has a very hard, protective layer of scales. The
trunkfish has no internal skeleton. Its outer layer of
thick tissue provides all the support the fish's body
needs.

Like many other types of fish, the trunkfish has an

                        As coral grows, it forms buds called polyps.

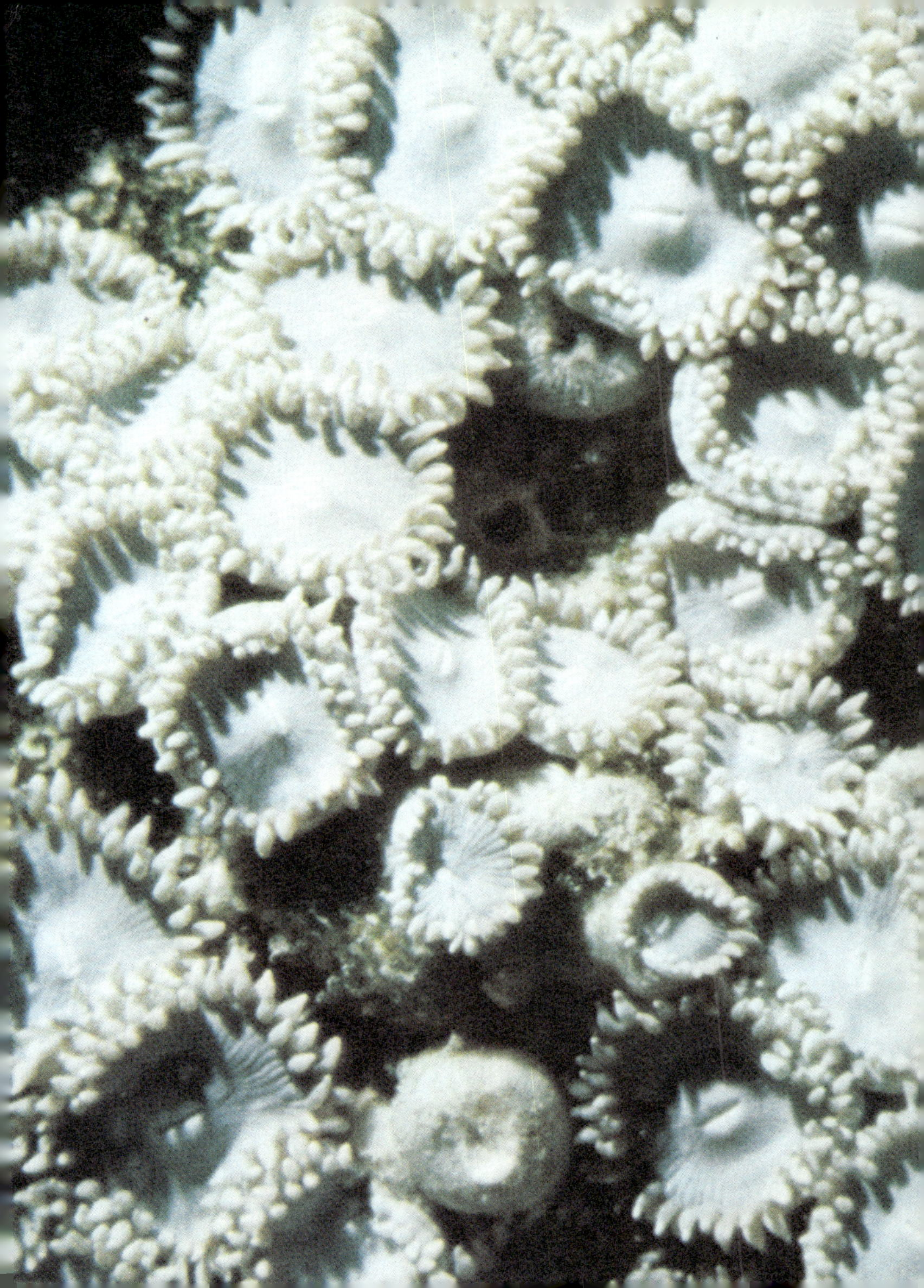

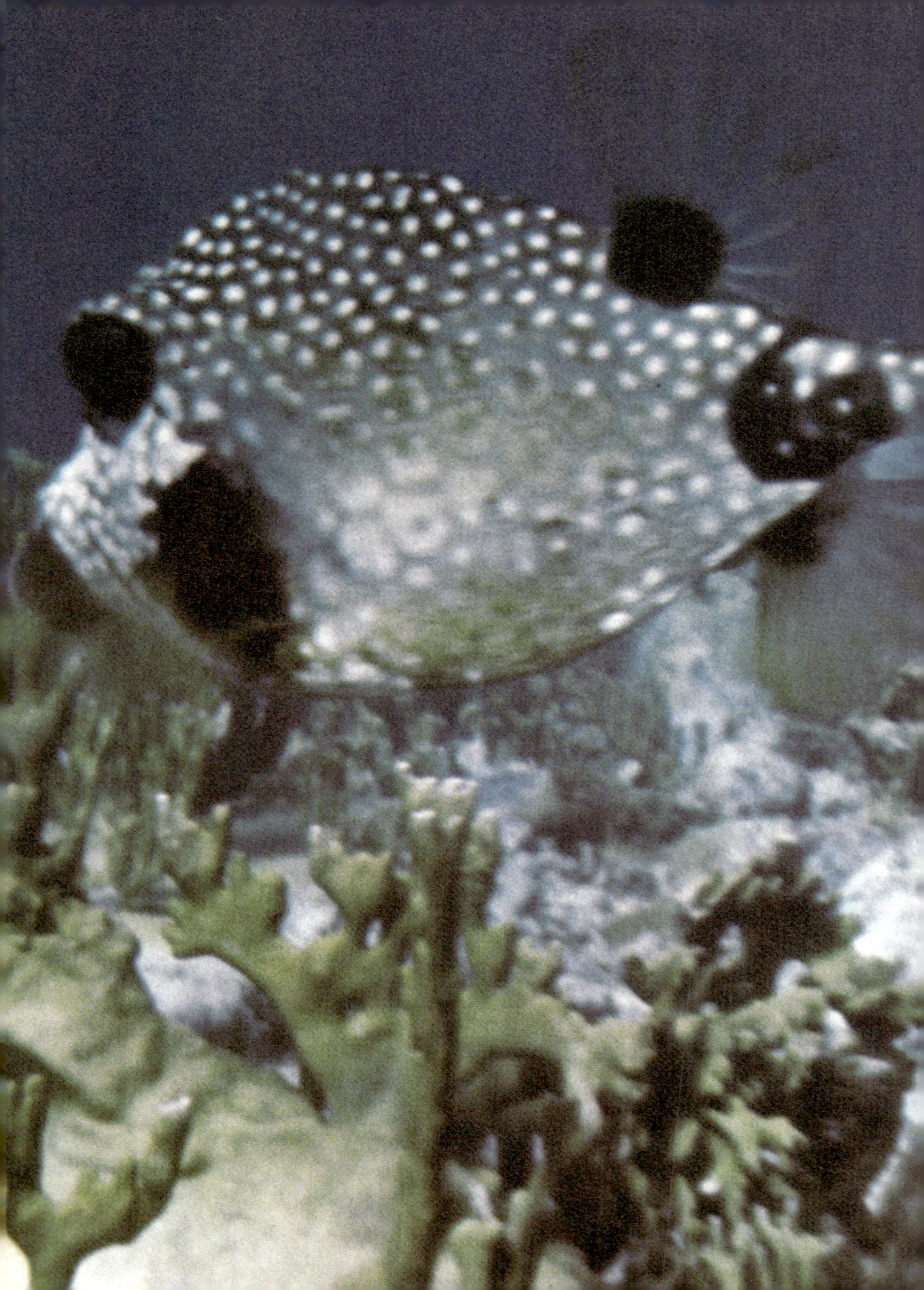

air bladder. This helps it float at various levels in the water. If the trunkfish wants to rise to the surface, it takes air in. The fish is then able to float upward. If it wants to go to the bottom, the trunkfish lets air out. This enables it to sink as desired.

The trunkfish likes to wander about coral reefs because of the abundance of plankton in the area. The trunkfish's coloring allows it to blend in with the coral and water. Enemies find it difficult to spot.

The trunkfish sacrifices speed and agility for its protective skin. The tail works hard to move the awkward body. The trunkfish weaves comically through the water. Its motions are rough and abrupt. It cannot turn as smoothly as other fish.

The underwater photographer finds a seemingly infinite number of organisms to photograph around coral reefs. None of these subjects is more colorful or interesting than the reef fish, which roam about alone or in schools.

The picture on page 34 shows a school of *reef fish* swimming under elkhorn coral. There are several reasons why these fish are brightly colored, and why they swim in schools. It would seem that these bright colors would make them highly visible to their enemies. But since coral is brightly colored, the fish can blend in and not be noticed. Coral also offers many nooks and crannies in which to seek refuge. The reef

The coloring of the trunkfish helps it to blend in with its surroundings.

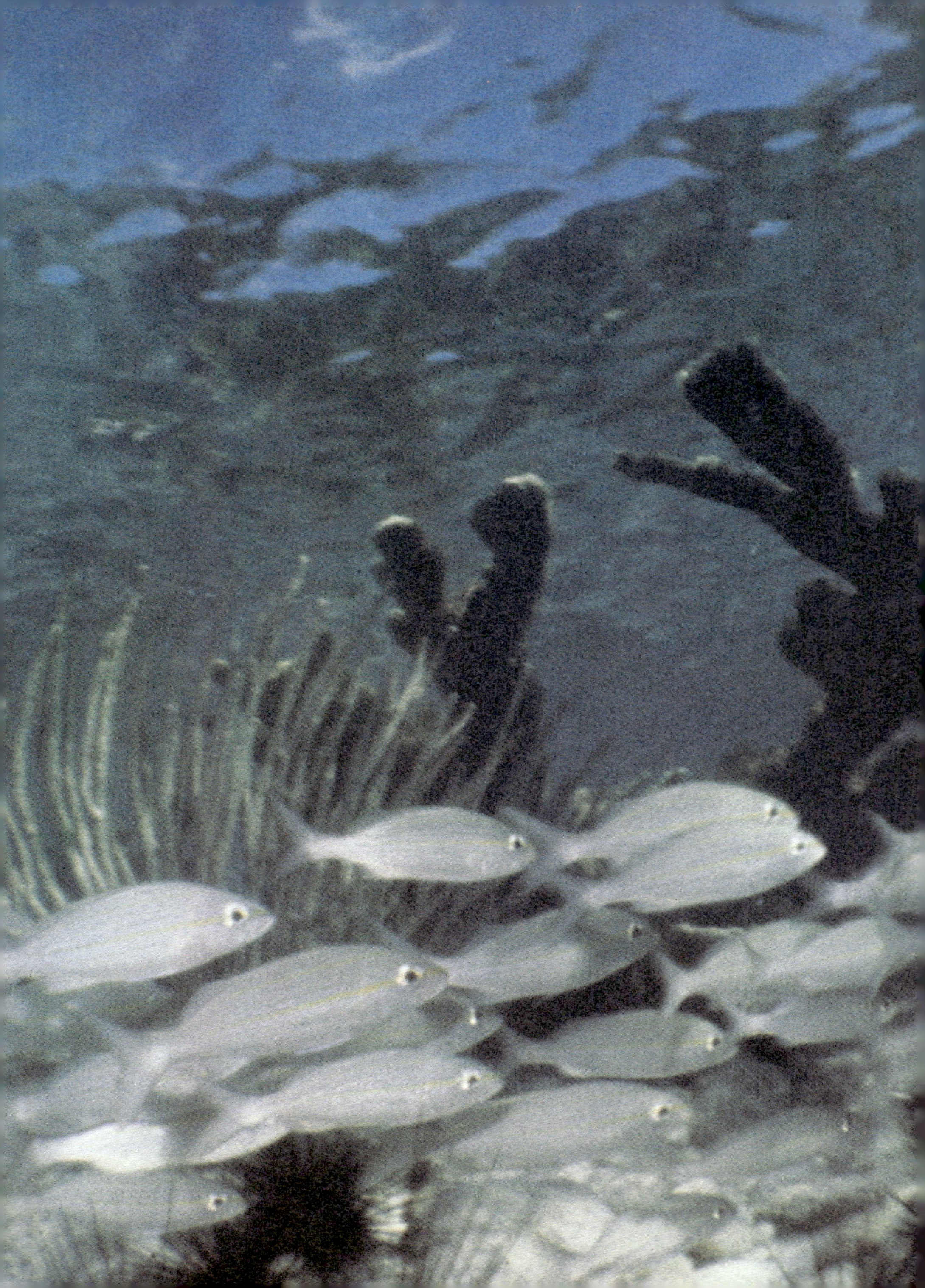

fish use their colors for protection when resting, laying eggs, or feeding.

Fish also use colors to warn attackers about poor-tasting flesh or poisonous spikes. Some fish have brightly colored horns and scales that give off poisonous venom under attack.

The colors shared by a group of fish help the group move and function as a unit. By sharing the same color, the fish can stay with each other as the group moves about in different directions. One of the amazing sights that greets the snorkeler is how well these schools of fish stay together. Their motions are rapid. They make many sharp dives and turns, but there appears to be no clearly designated leader. Each member of the school seems to help guide and protect the entire group.

Fish also use color to protect territories. All space on a coral reef is occupied. As you can imagine, there is much competition for space on a reef. A fish's bright colors help it to tell other fish that it is in control of an area. Space is so precious that some fish occupy a crevice only by day. Another fish takes the spot at night when the daytime occupants are out searching for food.

Fish also use color as part of the mating ritual. Males and females recognize mates by the colors displayed. It is one way nature ensures that fish will be attracted to one another and produce offspring.

The brightly-colored reef fish can hide in coral reefs.

The *queen angel* is just one fish that uses colors to defend its territory. The queen angel, like the one shown on page 37, swims about with rapid movements. It is not at all bashful. It displays its colors for all to see. This is its signal that an area is already being used for finding food. Enemies are warned not to attack by the queen angel's bright colors. The display of colors makes for an effective bluff.

The queen angel, like many other fish that live around coral reefs, has an unusual shape. This shape helps it to survive. The queen angel's broad, flat sides allow it to enter narrow areas in search of food. Its small mouth is equipped with teeth made for scraping rocks and for plucking small fish out of holes in the coral. The queen angel also scrapes away and eats plankton and algae found on hard surfaces.

The queen angel demonstrates how certain sea creatures can support each other's survival. By eating algae, it keeps the coral reef free from harmful growth and bacteria. If the queen angel did not perform this task, decay and disease would harm the coral, slowing its growth or killing it.

The *bristle starfish* is also found along shorelines and coral reefs. There are many types of starfish. Most have five arms. These arms have tiny suction cups and prickly needles. Some starfish eat clams and scallops. A starfish will first engulf a shellfish. Then it will pry the shell open and eat the meat inside.

36   The broad, flat shape of the queen angel fish enables it to swim in narrow places between rocks and coral.

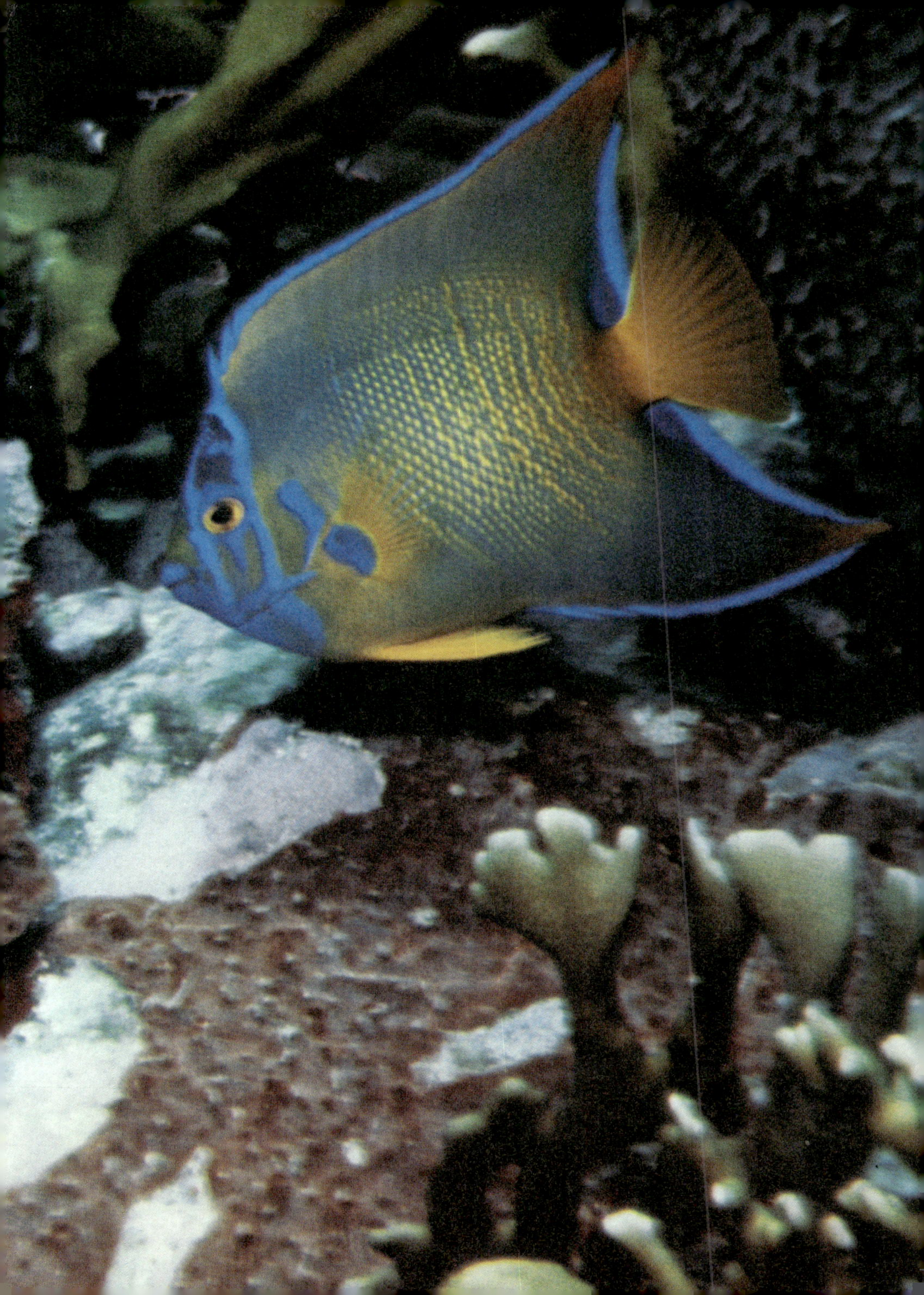

Some starfish feed off coral and organisms called sponges. If you look closely at the top picture on page 39, you can see a bristle starfish wrapped around a sponge. The starfish uses its suction cups to get a firm grip, and then makes holes in the sponge's body with its spikes. The starfish then draws food from the sponge through these holes.

Although starfish feed on useful forms of sea life, they are usually kept in check by other fish who feed on the starfish. Therefore, starfish are a problem only in areas where nature has been disturbed. For example, where fishing fleets have wiped out great numbers of starfish-eating fish, starfish flourish without check. They destroy entire clam beds and coral reefs. Undisturbed, nature maintains a balance of undersea life by allowing for a huge variety of living creatures.

The small, quick shrimp is another important link in the undersea food chain. The *banded coral shrimp* is pictured on the bottom of page 39, but there are many different types of shrimps. Most shrimps are only a few inches long. They are supported by long legs. Shrimps can scurry along the ocean floor in search of food. They are scavengers. They pluck plankton and algae from the ground. They also eat the food left over by other fish.

So great is the competition for food on the ocean floor, that shrimps could not survive without their long

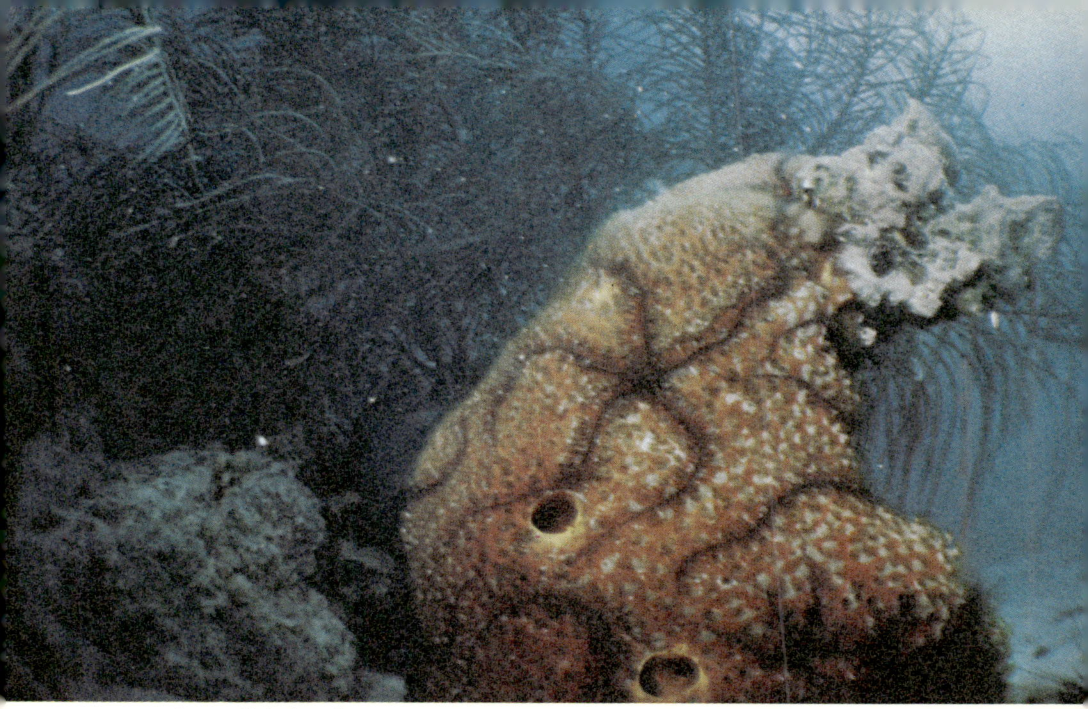

A starfish feeds on a sponge.

A banded coral shrimp searches for food on the ocean floor.

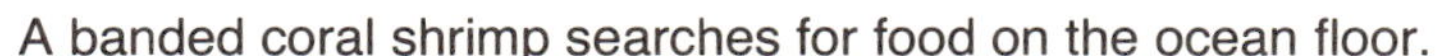

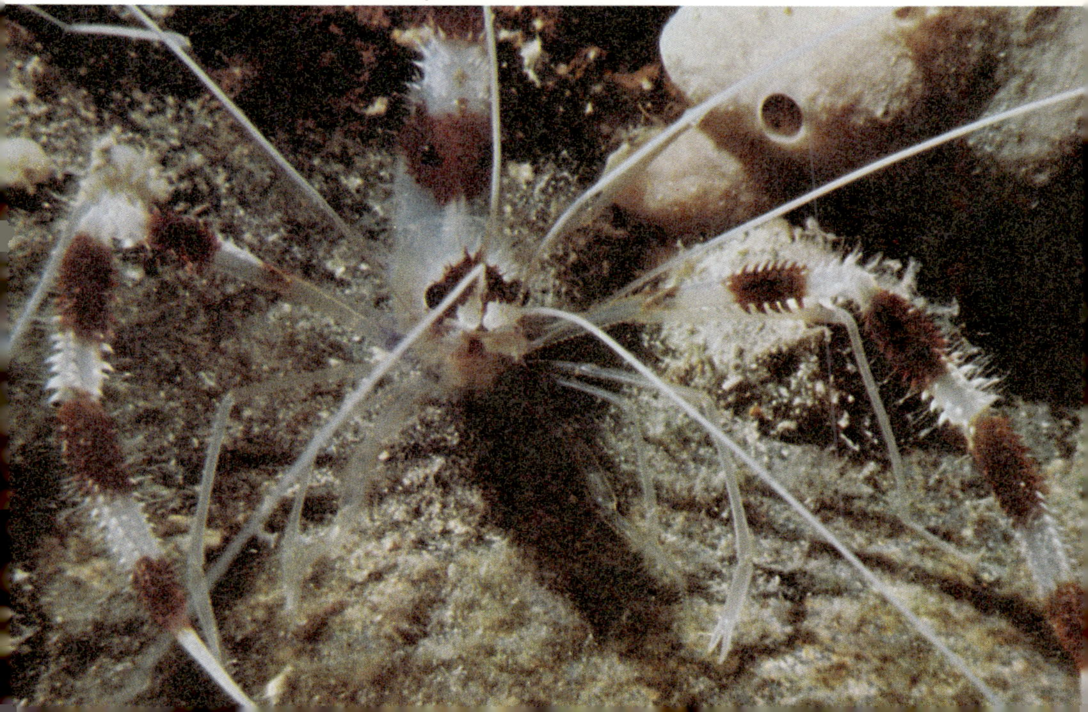

legs and sensitive feelers. Shrimps use their feelers to locate food on the dark ocean bottom.

Shrimps, in turn, help keep the ocean floor free of waste. They also serve as food for many other species of sea life. Of course, they are also prized as a food by human beings. Fossil remains prove that shrimps have existed on Earth for millions of years. Shrimps are a prime example of how the natural order of life in the ocean leaves nothing wasted. Every creature seems to have a specific function in this "other" world.

The delicate-looking tentacles pictured on page 41 belong to a *sea anemone*. The sea anemone's tentacles help this strange-looking creature to catch its food. Sea anemones are attracted to coral reefs and shallow waters for the same reason as most of the other reef inhabitants—the many kinds of food they can find there.

The tentacles of anemones certainly look graceful, but they are also deadly to small fish and crabs. The anemone uses its tentacles to sting fish or crabs that swim nearby. The tentacles inject a chemical that paralyzes the victim. Then the sea anenome slowly digests its prey.

Sea anemones attach themselves to coral or to the sea floor. Yet anemones are not stationary. They creep about the ocean floor in search of a good area to catch food. They also move from place to place searching for the right spot to reproduce.

     The sea anenome uses its tentacles to paralyze crabs and fish that swim by.

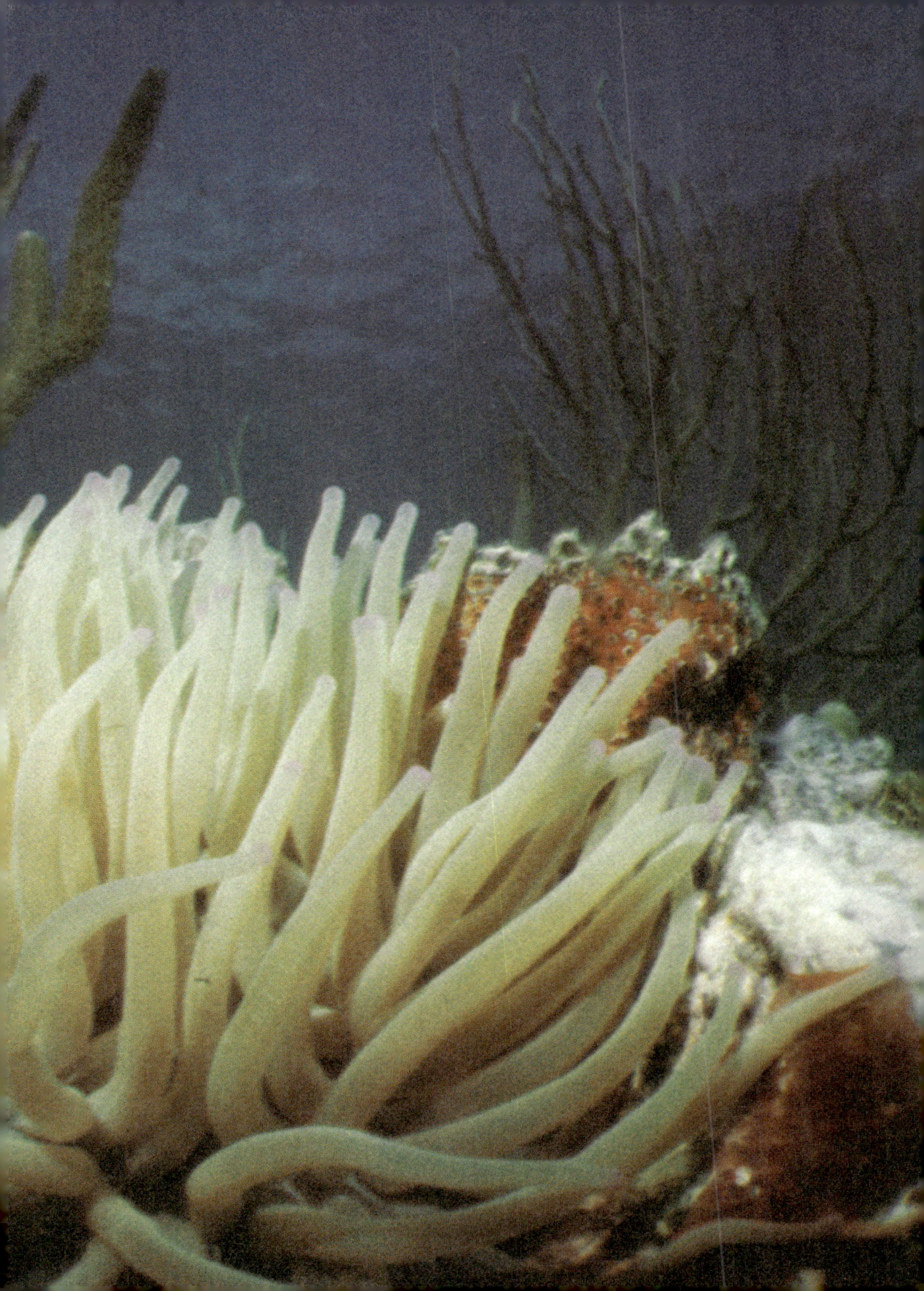

If you look closely at the picture on page 43, you will see a tiny shrimp perched on an anemone's tentacles. Shrimp often live on anemones. They find plankton and algae attached to the tentacles. Anemones do not eat these shrimp. It is almost as if the anemone senses that the shrimp is cleaning the tentacles of foreign material. This is yet another example of how living things depend on each other in the underwater world.

Sponges are another form of life that snorkelers and photographers find in shallow ocean waters. Sponges like those on page 44 are one of the most primitive forms of life found on earth. As with other organisms under the sea, there are many types of sponges. Each has its own shape and color patterns.

Sponges are simply a cluster of individual cells. They do not have a brain or nervous system. Sponges have tiny holes all over their outer layers. When water enters these holes, sponges filter out food particles. Sponges also grow tiny hairs that move large quantities of water into the openings in their bodies.

Sponges are stationary. Rather than move about, they anchor themselves to the ocean floor with grasslike threads. Sponges usually grow on rocky shelves near the shore. Here, water currents send a steady stream of food through the sponges. Many shellfish and other creatures can be found around sponges. They eat the algae that become attached to the sponge's skin. Because sponges attract so many

Shrimps feed on the plankton and algae that live on anenome tentacles.

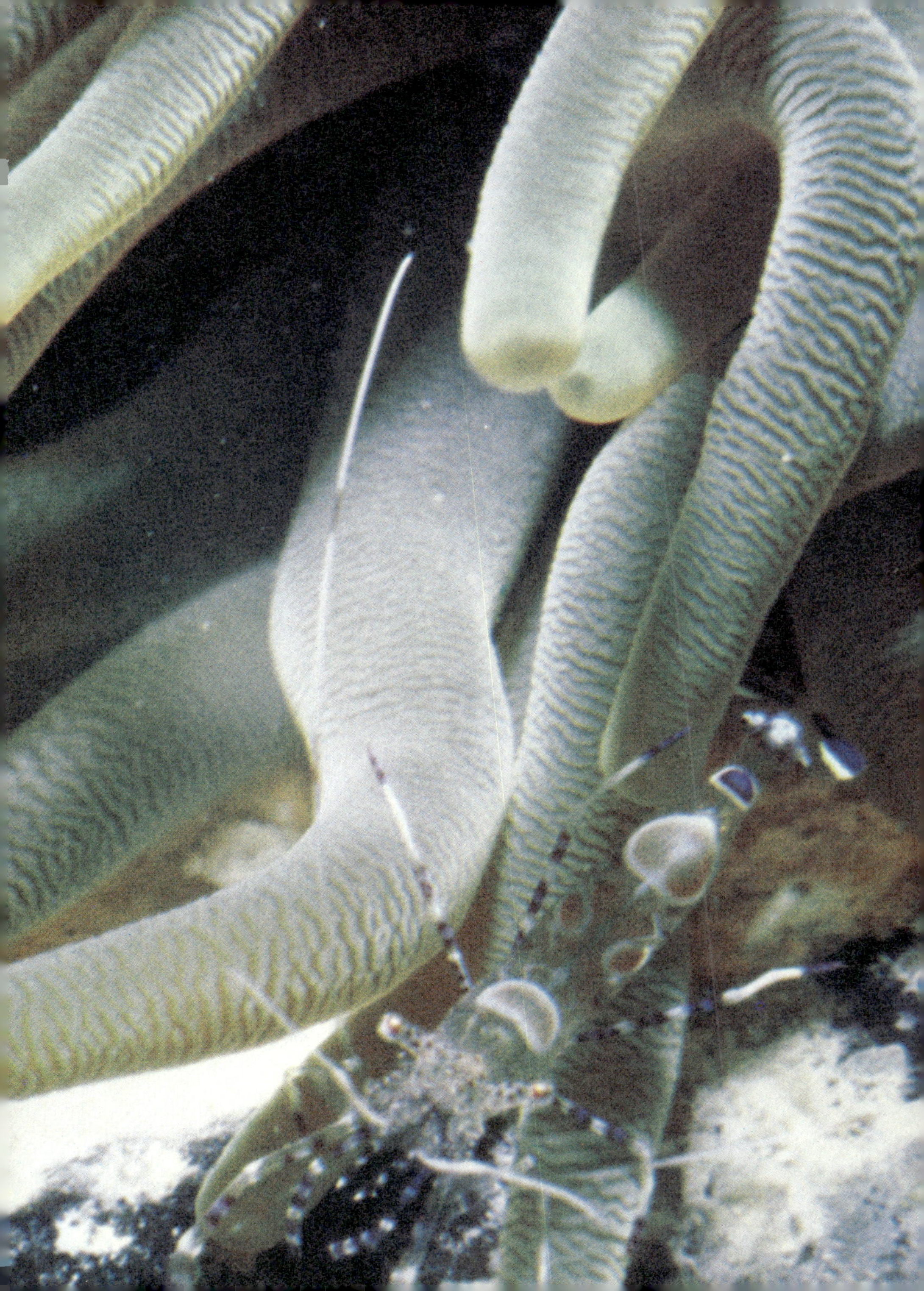

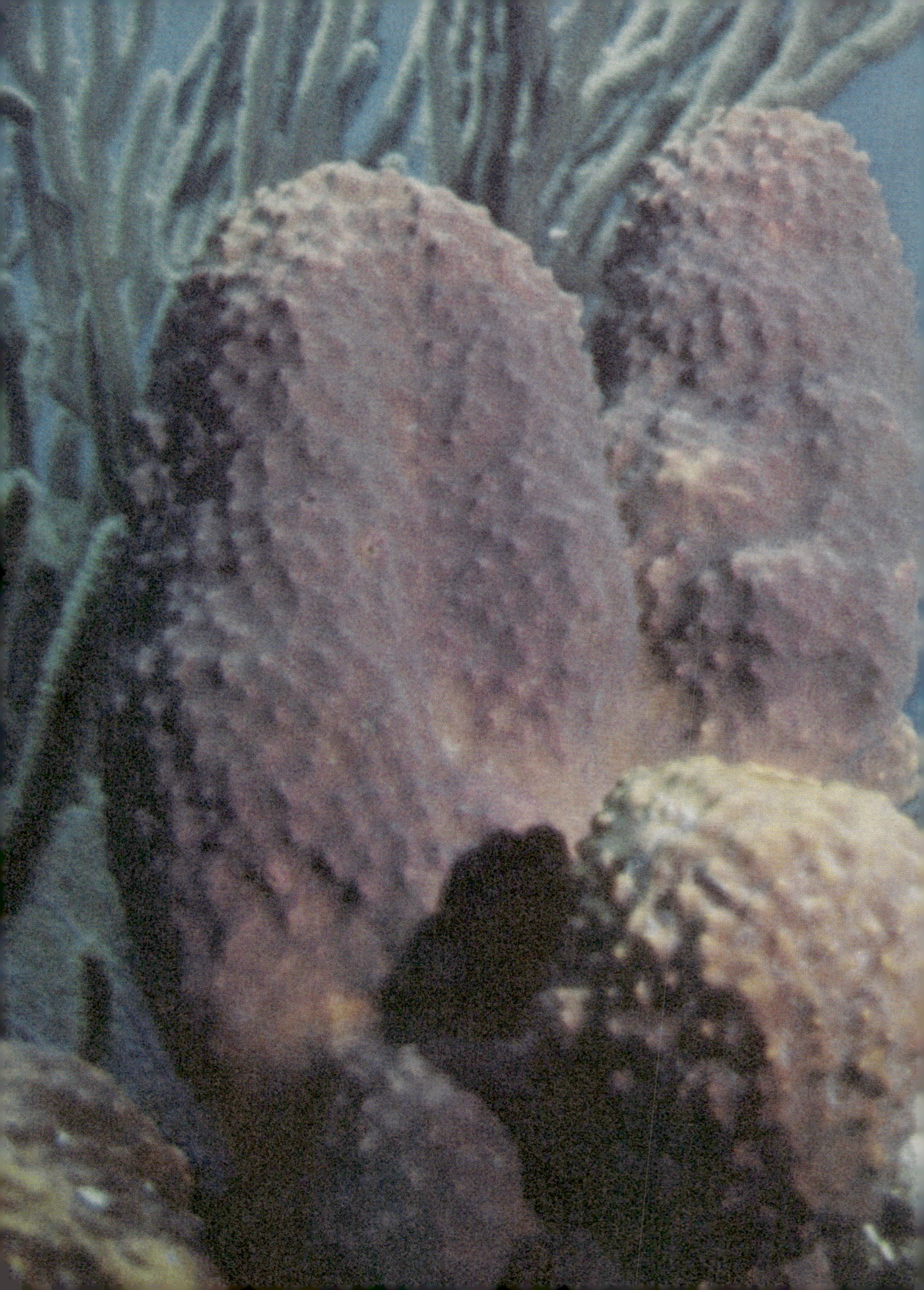

forms of sea life, they are often favorite subjects for
underwater photographers.

You probably have seen many earthworms. But have
you seen some of the many kinds of ocean worms that
do not look like earthworms at all? One of these is the
feather duster worm. The feather duster worm, pictured
on page 46, is another inhabitant of the coral reef. This
worm attaches itself to coral and grows silky strands
that look like feathers. Like the sponge, feather dusters
also filter water through their bodies to find food.
Water passes through the delicate silken flowers.
Microorganisms get caught in these strands. The
feather duster then sticks its head out to feed on the
plankton caught in its graceful petals. Snorkelers
around a coral reef are sometimes lucky enough to see
the feather duster worm in action.

The picture of the feather duster worm gives you an
idea of the graceful designs that can be seen in the
underwater world. Snorkeling is the easiest way to
witness such beauty in the living world of the ocean.

Underwater photographers also have a fine view of
activities along the water's surface. By swimming
silently and slowly, a snorkeler can spy many birds, for
example, that live around the water. Such is the case
with the bird pictured on page 47. This photograph
was taken by a snorkeler shooting from the water's
surface. The bird in the picture is called a *boobie*. The
boobie makes its nest on islands and on rocky slopes

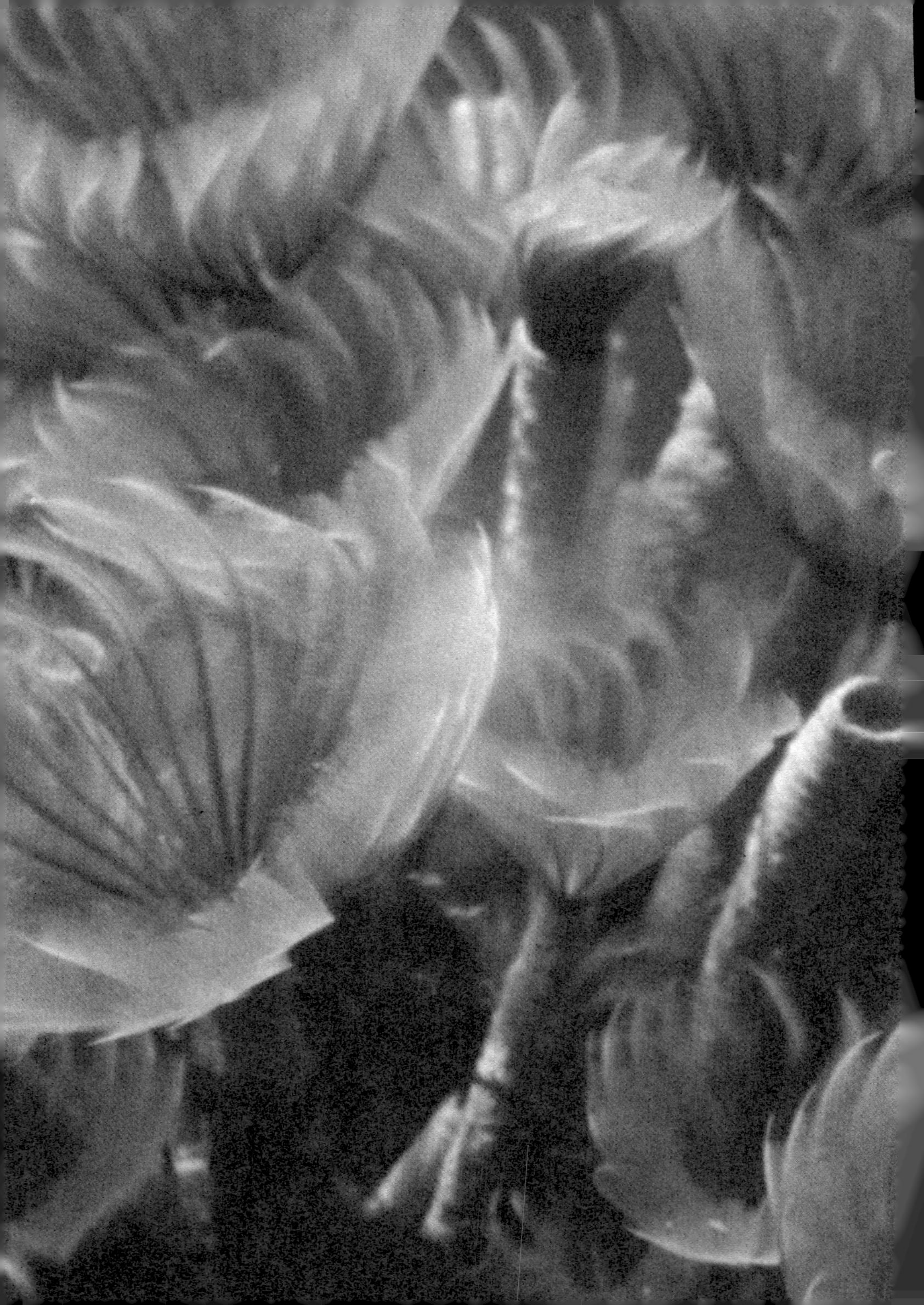

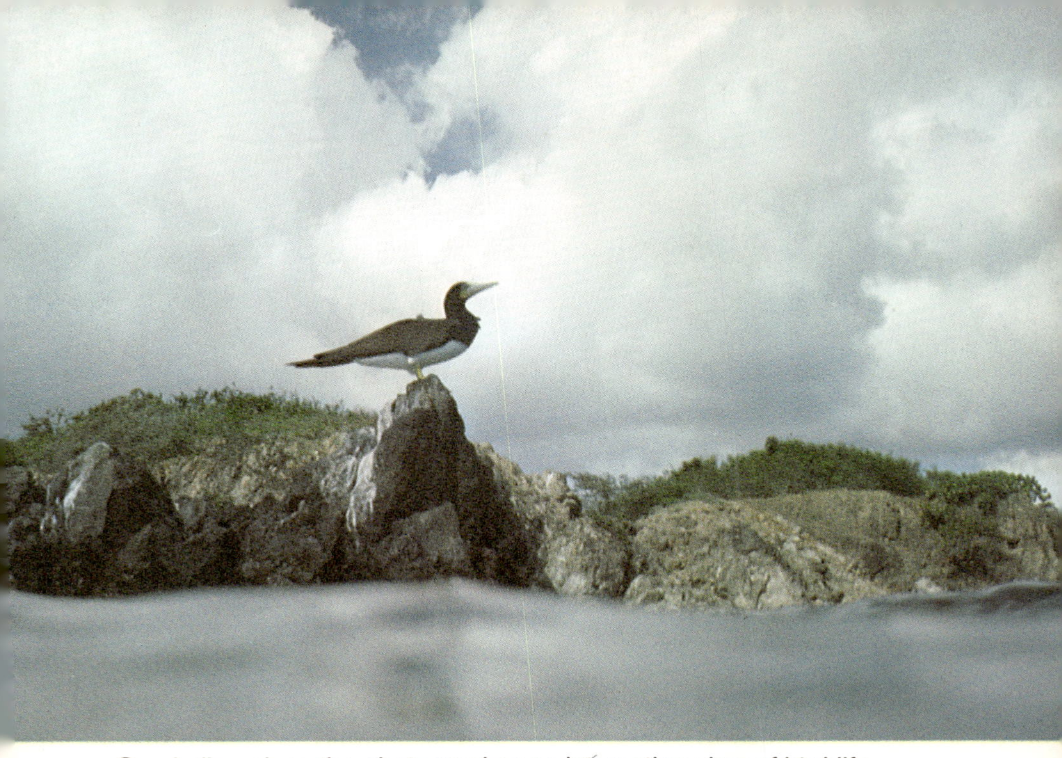

Snorkeling gives the photographer an interesting view of bird life, too.

near the ocean shore. It has webbed feet that help push it through the water. Boobies catch fish by circling about 50 feet above the water. When they see movement, they plunge toward the water at great speed. Just before they hit the water, they close their wings. This allows them to dive through the water with great force. A boobie will sometimes dive through as much as 40 feet of water, and come back up far from the original point of entry. The boobie's screeching dive can be one of the most impressive sights in the "other" world called the ocean.

The odd-looking feather duster worm looks nothing like an earthworm.

There is much for the snorkeler to see in the underwater world. People can enter this world with ease, provided they have the right equipment and know some basic techniques. In this book, we have taken a look at a few of the sights that greet explorers in the underwater world. There are many more things to discover, whether you snorkel in the ocean, a river, or a lake.

Snorkeling is more than just a relaxing hobby. It helps you see how nature works to help all creatures survive. The underwater photographer can capture strength, grace, and beauty on film. This hobby brings a person close to the workings of nature in a most enjoyable way.

Perhaps one day you will venture into this undersea world. Marvelous riches await you. The undersea world is part of the chain of life that helps keep our world healthy, stable, and beautiful.